MW01282405

NO FILTERS -
My journey with Dementia

By

Beth M. Ribesky

CreateSpace
Independent Publishing
2016

Published by Beth M. Ribesky
Printed by CreateSpace Independent
Publishing 2016
Charleston, SC, USA
© 2016 Beth M. Ribesky

ISBN: 1516962230
ISBN-13:9781516962235

Cover: "Lake Michigan: Journey to peace. . ."
Photographic Art by Beth M. Ribesky
Muskegon, Michigan

Book Design: Beth M. Ribesky

Copy-editor: Julia L. George, Creative Editor
Heritage Writings, Muskegon, Michigan

First Edition
March, 2016

DEDICATION

This journal is dedicated to my Mom and her courageous battle with the "Monster".

**No Filters –
My journey with Dementia**

de men tia

dəˈmen(t)SH(ē)ə/ *noun*

MEDICINE

1. A chronic or persistent disorder of the mental processes caused by brain disease or injury and marked by memory disorders, personality changes, and impaired reasoning.

synonyms: Mental illness,
madness, insanity, derangement, lunacy
"her failing memory is not necessarily a symptom of dementia"

What a horrible "medical" definition.

"My mom was not mentally ill, mad, insane, deranged or a lunatic. That is what the "monster" represents, not the unwilling participant that Dementia grabs hold of".

-Beth M. Ribesky

TABLE OF CONTENTS

Section Three – Little things: Time to share some hopefully helpful tips in caring

1.   Animals are amazing
2.   Reminders
3.   The calm of laundry detergent
4.   The day
5.   New items
6.   Patience

Final Thoughts –

ACKNOWLEDGMENTS

I want to thank everyone that has touched my life the last 6 years as Mom and I went through this journey. That would include all the doctors, nurses, nurse aides and any other staff that helped. Thank you to all of my friends that just sat and listened to me the times I had complete meltdowns and although they knew there was nothing they could do, they listened.

I also want to thank the handful of people that I gave this journal to that read it and encouraged me to keep writing even if it meant crying each and every time I sat down to write and remember what happened. I am forever grateful and love you all.

And thank you Mom, I love you.

No Filters* -
My journey with Dementia

Background

Mom . . .

My Mom was one of the kindest most generous people you would probably ever want to meet. She has had a million friends over her lifetime, close friendships with co-workers (white, black and Hispanic), not one racist bone in her body, never referring to anyone in a certain way because of their ethnicity. I remember her taking me to dinner at a Latin American Club when I was growing up just to experience the culture, and it is a great memory I have with me to this day. I sat with a bunch of Hispanic people who many people would have thought of as scary by looking at them, but they taught me how to speak some Spanish and learn to count up to 7 in Spanish. I still look back on that and smile because it was my real Mom just enjoying people like she used to. So as you read through this and start to see the dementia kick in you will understand how our loved ones (their personalities) are taken from us and how they are truly never the same; how all of the sudden they seem to have "No Filters" on what they say . . . they just speak their mind.

Anyways, Mom.

My Mom.

My Mom was more active then most of my friends well into her mid 70's. Didn't fully retire until age 76. She bowled twice a week, had the best vegetable garden in Lakeside, loved her flower garden and was a bartender at the Vikings Lodge where she was a member for 40 years, worked tons of parties there and seemed like she was going 100 mph 7 days a week 24 hrs a day. She divorced my Dad when I was 8, worked full time and raised 4 kids on her own never complaining once, yeah, she was something.

Please remember as you read this that this is not a typical book, this is my journal/experiences over the course of 6 years as a caregiver to my Mom as she started with the first signs of Dementia at age 78 up until the end of her journey. Therefore it's written more in a journal form with grammar errors as would be presented if I just wrote it out by hand, in other words, it's not perfect . . . as in real life.

Memories

Most of the best memories all of us kids have to this day are the parties at Mom's house, always the day before the holiday, for us to rest on the actual holiday . . . Memorial Day, 4ᵗʰ of July and Labor Day.

The Memorial Day party was always the start of summer. This party normally consisted of all the family with a few neighbors thrown in for a night of drinking, card playing and lots of laughs and memories, just a chance for all of us to get together.

The 4th of July party was more intense. A trip to the Indiana border for illegal fireworks a month before that triggered a full on family party with most of the neighborhood either coming to join us or just idly sitting by watching as my Mom's yard was engulfed in fireworks from the time the sun went down to well past midnight. A police scanner always in the background as we all listened when her house number was mentioned for a loud fireworks complaint at which time we would hear a quick shout out to "stop", then quickly turn all the lights off and watch as the police slowly drove by. Then when they were gone the "all clear" would be summoned and we would continue on with explosions and an occasional "brick" of firecrackers thrown in the middle of the street to really upset the neighbors that were calling the police on us, then another police scanner mention would come and all would be dark and quiet again as we watched the police drive by . . . oh, the memories.

The Labor Day party eventually turned into our "cholesterol party", deep fry city. We had deep fryers going on the deck and in the middle of the yard offering up fish, french fries, deep fried cauliflower, onion rings, mushrooms, you name it we deep fried it. At the last party we even tried some candy bars (well before it was as famous as it is around the fairgrounds now) all in good fun with all the family attending. Mom beaming from ear to ear because we were all there with her grand kids in tow to just celebrate the day together and be silly, always with the sound of a horse shoe game echoing in the background as my brothers bet against each other and laughed.

Mom held on to these parties as long as she could. We all have such cool memories of these as well as a lot of the neighbors and they still say "remember when" when I see them to this day. Yes, my mom was considered one of the "cool moms" on the block. She stayed "young" even as she was aging a long, long time.

She even started working with Meals on Wheels at age 72 and said it was fun working with "old people", she said in a very young state of mind until right around age 76.

Being the youngest of the bunch here (Mom had me later in life when she was 33 and my brothers when she was 19, 24 & 25 — yes I was a "mistake") so I don't have as many memories with my mom as my brothers do about which I am a bit jealous, but they don't have the memories later in life with Mom that I have, even being in her clouded state of mind at times. This can never be taken from me and looking back now, I wouldn't change a thing with the relationship we developed later in her life, that trusted loving relationship of a mother and her daughter as we both knew things were changing in her world that she had no control over. Scary at times and oh so funny at times I can still see her shake her head as she would say, "oh, Bethie" –and we would both giggle.

Last full on laugh I had with my Mom was at Meijer's grocery store, looking at birthday cards with her for my oldest brother. Mom was in pretty good spirits that day, some confusion, but not too bad. So as I walked down the aisle from her looking at cards this bright yellow card grabbed my eye with Sponge Bob and as I started singing out loud *"Sponge Bob"* to the other end of the aisle I hear her singing back *"Square pants"* I busted out laughing and said "do you know who that is?" And she said "of course" to which we both started full on laughing. Pretty dang cool for an 83 year old!

Dementia**

What a crazy thing to have happen to someone, a bummer is more like it. There are different types of dementia and I quickly learned and the "type" my Mom had is considered dementia induced by alcoholism, so this is a tricky one. Dementia is tricky enough then add the stimulant of alcohol on top of that, well, it makes for interesting times, and all I could say in the beginning before it got "dark" was let the adventures begin.

**Please note, in no way am I making light of any of this, I was her primary care giver at that point, but making light of things that happened and sharing stories of what she had done to me or situations we have been in seemed to make people laugh so it's time to share them with you and hopefully if you are going thru something similar you can have an out loud laugh and know you are not alone in this world, especially if you've experienced similar things.

So, here goes . . .

NO FILTERS – *My journey with Dementia*

Section One – The beginning, yeah, it's funny alright . . .

1. I'm going to jail

We live in Michigan, so as you are probably aware we get lots of snow here and it's no fun to shovel. Easiest way to get rid of the snow is with a snow blower and with a very independent 76 yr old woman that's perfect, right? Wrong.

So, I'm out getting my hair cut and I get this awful phone call from my mother that she has fallen down her basement stairs, all 12 stairs and I'm thinking "oh my God, she broke her hip" and all she said is "there is blood everywhere and the neighbor is taking me to the hospital, hurry up and get there". So no broken hip — whew. Least of my worries for what is coming.

I get to the hospital in record time as she is being admitted and she looks awful, like someone has beaten the living daylights out of her, she completely ripped all the skin off the top of both of her hands, is bruised on her back, head, right leg and has a huge gash on her foot. How she didn't break a bone is a miracle, we are counting our blessings right now.

So the nurse comes in and does her normal stuff while admitting someone, blood pressure, temp, etc. and starts to ask the questions from the form in front of her (which later I found out was in regards to Elderly Abuse):

Nurse - "Ok Norma, I have a few questions for you, do you feel scared at this time?"

Mom - "Yes," (I'm thinking, who wouldn't after a fall like that at her age?) so the nurse makes a note staring at me.

Nurse - "Does anyone ever hurt you?" "Or has anyone hurt you in the past?"

Mom - looking at me, "Only my daughter." — as she starts to snicker —

Me - "What? Mom be honest here she needs to do her job."

Mom - "I am," then she starts laughing. (I'm thinking, oh, my God, they think I hurt her.)

Mom - "They know I'm kidding."

Nurse - eyeing me at this point. . .

Me - "Mom, she doesn't know you or your sense of humor, it's important right now that you be honest with her or they are going to get a police officer in here and take me to jail for elderly abuse."

Mom - "Ok, she doesn't hit me and this wasn't her fault. I was kidding when I said that."

Nurse - still glaring at me as she is writing, "Ok Norma, but we still have to make a note on your chart to cover what you actually said here today in case we need it at a later date if you get injured again." Great, now it's on the record that she may have an abusive daughter. All the while she is laughing thinking this is hilarious.

And the final question:

Nurse - "Do you feel threatened at all at this time by anyone around you?" as she is staring at me.

Mom - "No, not right now."

Me - "What? I have never threatened you."

Mom - "I know, I was kidding."

Oh, my God...

So in comes the doctor to assess her injuries. She is sent down to have x-rays just to be safe. Nothing is broken, thank God. She ends up with numerous bruises, stitches in her right foot and huge bandages on her hands that we will have to tend to twice a day for the next couple of months. Then we are told skin grafts will be needed, so I have my work cut out for me for a few months tending to bandages and doctor's appointments as she heals. So we are released to take her home, and again, thank God nothing was broken and she is still alive.

And I'm thinking this whole "my daughter beat me up" is behind me – ummm – no, silly, silly me.

The night went ok, she, of course, was extremely sore and we had one injury that just would not stop bleeding (thanks to blood thinner medicine people take as they get older), so the next morning we decide to head into our family doctor to have him take a look.

Both hands are bandaged like a boxer, two white mitts and she is now turning black and blue on her head and neck where everyone can see and of course not walking well because she is sore from the fall, but we manage to get her into the lobby of the doctor's office, the packed doctor's office I might add who all turned to look when we walked in – great.

So as we are sitting there she has both her hands up and everyone is staring at her at this point and this nice little elderly lady said, "Oh, my, gosh, what happened to you honey?"

Mom looked at me and I said you might as well tell her everyone is wondering,
she looks at me, grins and says, " My daughter beat me up. "Everyone gasped. "Really?" I heard a man's voice say behind me "Really? This daughter?" (oh shit, now I'm going to get beat up) and she laughed and said "No, but that's what I told them at the hospital, it was so funny." Ok, maybe jail would be easier at this point.

The moral of the story, do not try to take your snow blower down into your basement when the weather man said it's going to get really cold and snow because you think it won't start sitting in the garage, you might fall down 12 stairs trying to carry it and get hurt really bad.

The good news, with constant bandage care we had her healed up with no skin grafts needed in 6 weeks, she was an amazingly tough woman with good strong Swedish bones.

2. Sometimes duct tape is needed

We weren't actually told we were dealing with dementia until she was nearing 78. She had some mix ups on her medications that she normally was 100% on top of and some confusion and anger was setting in. My mom worked in the accounting field and was amazing with numbers and keeping books (checkbook, taxes, etc.) and all of a sudden she couldn't remember the simplest math so being a bit concerned off to the doctor we go to get her checked out.

We are very fortunate that she has had the same family doctor and nurse for the last 35 years so they were very aware of how she normally was and that there was a change now. And the receptionist has been the same for almost as many years so long story short here, they are all "on board" that we may have a problem.

So we are off to the doctor. Mom is angry with me because she thinks nothing is wrong and doesn't want to see anyone. Right now in her eyes I am an awful daughter. This is going to be an interesting day. Quiet ride there, she won't talk to me because right now I am the enemy.

We arrive at the doctor's office and still no talking, not even a comment on the weather, perfect. I'm thinking she probably won't even talk to the doctor today.

Sitting quietly in the lobby of the doctor's office I can just see those wheels in her head turning when the receptionist walks by and says "Hi Norma, so good to see you," to which my mother has no reply. . .and just as she (the receptionist) is almost out of our hearing range Mom says "Can you believe how much weight she has gained since she got married?" and of course with the shock of what she just said I said "What?" and she had to repeat it. Of course she (the receptionist) heard it and motioned to me, "It's ok," I couldn't apologize enough. I said "Mom, that isn't nice and you can't say things like that" to which she looked at me and said "well it's true". . .

The nurse calls us in, "Good afternoon Norma," she said, no reply from Mom, she's still angry with me. Get her weighed, blood pressure taken and then it goes like this:

Nurse – "So what brings you in today Norma?"
Mom – "My daughter, she hates me."
Me – "What?"
Nurse – "Oh, I don't believe that, now really what's got you coming in to see us today?"
Mom – Silence.
Nurse – "Ok, let's have Doc come in and chat with you. Beth, can you come outside for a minute?"
Mom – "Go ahead, tell them I need to be locked up and put away."

Not saying a word I quietly walk out and meet with the nurse and the doctor and explain what has been going on and back in the room with Mom we go:

Doctor - "So Norma, how are we feeling today?"
Mom – Silence.
Doctor - "Anything we need to talk about?"
Mom – Silence.
Doctor - "So Beth would you like to fill me in on what brings you in here with your Mom today?"
Mom – Angrily— "She hates me so I'm sure she has plenty to tell you."
Me – "Mom that isn't true, we're here to talk about how you're feeling and what we can do to make things better and easier for you."
Mom – "See, she wants to lock me up. Oh, I just want to die."
Doctor – "And eventually you will as we all will, but until then let's see what we can do to get you feeling better right now."
Mom – Speechless.
Me – . . .thinking what a great answer, laughing inside the whole time.

Long story short we decided she needed some blood work and we're going to change some medications, add one for memory issues (which we decide to tell her is an extra vitamin so she won't fight us on an additional med each day) so now we need to go have her blood drawn. Normally easy thing? Nope, not today. . .

In the car we go, her arms are folded and she is even angrier. All I hear about on the way to the hospital is how the doctor only talked to me like she wasn't in the room and she didn't appreciate it and how she was never going with me again. Damn, I'm tired at this point.

We get to the lab and she is fine going in, get the blood drawn and on the way out there are more people waiting as she decides to make a scene. "Don't go in there, they have taken all my blood and I can hardly see straight, they took 5 pints" (5 vials) as I look to a horrified child in the waiting room who starts crying "Mommy, don't make me go in there." Of course her Mom that was with her was beyond angry because those of us with children all know how difficult it is to get a child to have blood drawn let alone have a senior citizen freak them out even more. All I can say is "I'm so sorry," and tell my Mom to knock it off and to go get into the car — and who's the parent here?

Quiet ride home, arms folded not a word until we walk in her door where she reluctantly eats half of a turkey sandwich at the kitchen table, then walks to her recliner (jacket still on) sits, folds her arms still angry and not 5 minutes later is sound asleep.

3. Afternoon appointments should be easier, right?

Time for another doctor's appointment, so I'm thinking if I can get a last appointment of the day without a full waiting room I should be safe from any harm her mouth can do at this point, right? Think again.

I've had a busy day at work, so I'm running a few minutes late. I pick mom up get her to the doctor's office, registered and sat down in the waiting room with one other woman (who happens to be African American) and only 10 minutes before her appointment. Whew, this should be a safe uneventful trip today, yeah! Mom is sitting quietly and even though I can see her wheels turning in that brain of hers she hasn't said a word, so far so good. Other lady goes in, we're next . . . no problem.

We get in the room, nurse does her normal stuff, Mom is talkative, this is going to be fine today, until. . .

Nurse walks out and we are waiting for the doctor to come in. Walls are thin so you can hear some of what is going on in the next room, happens to be the African American woman that was in the waiting area with us. And out of the blue:

Mom - "Think I'm going to go for a ride this weekend up to Fremont."
Me – "Weather is supposed to be perfect, that sounds nice."
Mom – "Yeah, think I want to ride by that house where they found all that Ku Klux Klan stuff in that guy's attic years ago."

Me - "What?" (in total shock right now and in a panic hoping they couldn't hear us in the next room) "Wait don't say that again. Where, how . . . why would you say something like that right now?"
Mom - "I was just thinking."

In walks the Doctor and he patiently says "So thinking of going for a drive this weekend Norma?". . . please just shoot me now.

4.   Dinner out? What was I thinking? Apparently I wasn't.

Ok, birthday time for Mom –had the big party at 80 with all the family and that was great, quiet 81 and now we are at 82 and I thought it would be nice to take her out for a nice quiet dinner, she wanted just the two of us to go, "no fuss" as she put it, ok, I'm in, should be harmless— uh, oh.

We go to Red Robin, one of her favorite places because she can order any kind of hamburger she wants and she knows she will take half home for a meal later, so she is happy, this is going to be great.

After we are seated in walks a couple and yes they are a large couple and I'm not saying that is bad, I certainly have some weight to lose myself so I am never a judge of anyone. Mom notices them and doesn't say a word, just looks at me and grins like she wants to say something but I quick shake my head no and she leaves it at that, for now.

We order our dinner, waitress brings us our drinks and goes to get the order from the other couple, no problem. Our food comes out and so does the food for the other couple, and here we go.

Mom - "They sure ordered a lot of food."
Me - "Mom, please be quiet, people can hear you talk."
Mom - "Well they did."
Me - . . . trying desperately to change the subject.
Waitress - "How is everything, tasting good?"
Me - "Yes, everything is great."
Mom - Leans in to the waitress "Can you believe all the food that table ordered? My gosh that was a lot for two people."
Me - . . . embarrassed beyond words.
Waitress - "We have lots of tasty things on the menu so we are happy when people order lots of different things to try."
Me - Thinking what a great answer and it's over. . .nope.
Mom - "Well, it does take a lot of food to maintain weight like that."
Me - Oh, my God, where can I hide?

At this point I'm embarrassed beyond belief, praying they didn't hear what she said, but by the burning looks I could just feel coming at me I knew they heard at least something. All I can think is hurry up and eat so we can get out of here.

Waitress - "Would you ladies like any desert?"
Me: "No thank you, just the check please," thinking we can make a quick getaway before they are done with their meal.

And just as we are getting ready to get up they bring a chocolate cake desert to the table of our new friends and I look at my Mom whose mouth is already opened to say something and I say "Not a word, not one single word," and escort her out the door. Again . . . who's the parent here?

5.   Neighbors: "She needs to move, now!"

So everyone has an elderly lady in their neighborhood that they talk about, right? Well, my Mom used to be the "cool Mom" on the block, she raised three boys and myself and we all know what kind of mischief boys can bring, but she weathered through just fine and has been in the same house for the past 58 years, so she has a good handle on the neighborhood and how it "use to be." Here is her description of her neighbors when I would see her each day and she had something to tell me.

Her neighbors (in her mind now) are as follows:

Rental house on the left—three units—long haired guy downstairs doesn't work and she's sure we are supporting him and his son so he should move. Now mind you, the economy here in Michigan is awful and the poor guy probably lost his job. Other two tenants are fine, so far.

House across the street — a cast of characters — and she has "nicknames" for them. First off she calls it "the felon house", dad is in prison, son is in prison, wife "Big Momma" lives there with her daughter who dates a Mexican (that's why she said the door needs to be locked). . .what? She has never been scared of anyone of any race before. Younger daughter that lives there had a baby out of wedlock. That's a whole other issue, about which I remind her "Ummm, weren't you pregnant when you got married?" To which she replied, "Yes, and all you kids have the same father" — unreal. House kitty corner from her, "colored people" moved in. Colored people? Again from my mom who has never been racist, I just replied, "Mom, what color? -- blue, green, what?" She said "You know --colored people." Just shook my head and said, "Mom, we don't talk like that." She said "Ok." This is another sign that dementia is creeping in. For her to just say "Ok" like a young child is not like her at all.

6. A "slip" off the deck or a fall? Only the hospital knew the truth . . . and it went like this:

I'm at a friend's house about 100 miles away on a Saturday night thinking I had not one worry in sight because on Saturday nights one of my brother's always visits my Mom for a few hrs and I know she is alright — well, not so much on this night.

Shortly after 6 my brother calls me:
Brother – "Mom fell on the deck and I think she needs to go to the hospital."
Me – "What? How did that happen? Is she alright?"
Brother – "Not sure, but the second time she fell I think she hurt herself pretty bad."

Me – "The second time? How did you let that happen, twice?" And really, how does someone watch their 81 yr old mother fall and let her get up and somehow do it again?
Brother – No answer.
Me – "I'm on my way, but I'm out of town, so get her there and I will meet you at the hospital."
Brother – "Ok, but hurry, she looks bad."

Then I hear her in the background saying "Who are you" to my brother and I said put her on the phone.

Mom – "Hello?"
Me – "Hey Mom, heard you took a fall on the deck."
Mom –"Did I? --boy does my head hurt. This nice man is going to help me."
Me – . . . trying not to panic by her answer, "You mean your son?"
Mom – "No, I don't know who he is."
Me – "Can you put that nice man on the phone?"
Brother – "Yeah?"
Me – "What the hell happened over there?"
Brother – "I don't know I just got here."
Me – "Get her to the hospital and I will be there as soon as I can."

I made it home in just over an hr --95 on the expressway, not sure how the heck I didn't get a ticket but someone was looking over me for sure that night. The whole ride home all I can think of is she had a stroke or something major that she had fallen and now doesn't know my own brother so of course I am scared out of my mind as to what I'm going to walk into and here I go.

As I arrive at the hospital she is admitted already (thank God I don't have to go thru the questionnaire again) and I am taken right back to the room she has been put in the emergency room area and before I get there I can hear her talking to the doctor:

Doctor – "Norma, what happened to you tonight?"
Mom – "I'm not sure, but my daughter will be able to tell you when she gets here."
Brother – "Huh? She wasn't even there. Mom fell off the deck and I think she really got hurt on the second fall."
Doctor – "Norma, you fell on your deck twice tonight?"
Brother – "She fell *off* the deck."
Me – As I come charging in "What do you mean she fell *off* the deck? And twice?" Immediately he leaves. He knew I was angry.
Mom – Shaking her head, "Hi Bethie." Well, at least she knows who I am.
Doctor – Asks me to step outside "We are going to run some tests, we aren't quite sure what is going on but by the sounds of her symptoms and the way she is talking right now, with everything being slurred and not making much sense, she may have had a stroke."

I'm in a total panic right now thinking the absolute worst and my brother is nowhere to be found.

So they wheel Mom down to get some x-rays and I go hunting for my brother. He is in the waiting area where I confront him on what he thinks happened.

He said he has no idea and he doesn't want to talk to me, so I ask, "Were you guys drinking by chance?" No, he said he just got there and "found her like that." So I asked "If you just got there, how did you see her fall and see her fall twice?"--silence, he says nothing. Great, now I know there is more to this story.

Mom is back.

Doctor – "Norma, have you had any alcohol tonight?"
Mom – "No, I don't drink."
Me – "What? Yes she does."
Mom – "Ok, I drink with my son on Saturday nights, we have one drink each."
Brother – . . .zips out of the room.
Me – (angry at my brother but trying to keep it in check to help with what my Mom is going through). "Mom, how much did you drink tonight?"
Mom – "I haven't had a drink yet." (My brother is gone so I know better.)

Doctor leans in closer to me and asks me to step out of the room to talk.

Doctor – "Your Mom didn't have a stroke, (thank God, I'm thinking) your Mom's blood alcohol level is currently at 23.8, she is 3 times the legal limit --umm, she's hammered."
Me – "What?" --stunned, but grateful she did not have a stroke.

Doctor tells me we have a decision to make, if she continues to drink like this she can't be on the blood thinner medication she needs because if she fell and hit her head, she could bleed internally and she could stroke out or she can quit drinking, continue to take her blood thinner medication and be fine. Great, this is going to be a difficult discussion with her I can tell already.

They bandage her up, minor bruising on her legs, cuts on her arms and hands and send us on our way. Once again, thank God she didn't break anything.

We get her home, tucked in and of course she passes out. I tell my brother who I can hardly speak to civilly at this point that he needs to stay with her for the night and I will be there first thing in the morning.

I call Mom early the next morning before I go in to see her and she says, "What happened to me? Why do I have a hospital bracelet on?" Clearly she doesn't remember anything that happened so I tell her I will be there in 10 minutes to have a talk with her, she knows she's in trouble. My brother is gone, he is my second stop of the day.

We had a very "hard" discussion that morning and my Mom never had another drink (that I knew of) since then and it really made a difference in her medical condition. My brother of course didn't like me anymore because I took his "drinking buddy" away and has made the comment that "who am I to tell her what she can and can't do at her age?" – siblings – whatever.

7. Medication lost . . . stupid cat

So some visible confusion has now set in and a conversation the prior night was not making any sense so maybe we need a doctor's visit just to get the meds checked out for possible dosage changes. Mom is not happy about this and is sure I'm crazy (which by now she is probably right) but whether she likes it or not, we're going in just to check things out.

Drive isn't bad, Mom is okay today with going in so I'm thinking this one should be a breeze today, no surprises, just some questions answered on medications and we will be out of there. I had no idea.

It's routine for my Mom now that when she goes in, she brings all her medication bottles, she doesn't trust that I have them all labeled in my phone for the hospital visits or that the doctor has them in his computer so we carry a bag in with us each time and she makes sure I put them all on the counter so he can review them.

We get checked in with the nurse and here we go:

Nurse – "So Norma, what brings you in today"?
Mom – Bethie thinks I have some confusion, but I think she is confused.

Me - Huh? --questioning my own judgment at this point.
Nurse – "Ok, so do you have any concerns that you can think of right now or are we just checking your meds today?"?
Mom – "No concerns except that my cat has taken some of my medications and hid them."
Me – "um, what?" – she hasn't shared this with me yet.
Mom – "Oh that cat is hiding stuff on me."

Nurse – "So do we have some missing?"
Mom – "Yes, a whole bottle, I have looked everywhere and no sign of it, she hid it good."
Nurse – "Beth were you aware of this?"
Me – . . . stunned "No, first I have heard of it."
Nurse – "Ok, let's get Doc in here and see what he has to say."

Now I'm sitting there wondering how much stuff this cat has "hidden" from her that she is not sharing. So I have to ask, "does she hide stuff on you often?" To which mom replies "Yeah, she is really good at it too." – great, this is going to be an interesting conversation with the doctor.

Her cat got blamed for many things that day including hurting her all the time, the reason why she has all the dark spots on her arms, not that the blood thinner would ever cause that? Well, at least I didn't get blamed for those, that day that is.

8. Time for more tests — a whole day at the hospital — God help me

Ok, so now that we have confusion and added anger the doctor has decided we need to get the real testing done, all the tests to determine if we are dealing with Alzheimer's, so let's go have blood work done, an EKG for her rapid heartbeat, a CAT scan to check her brain, a sleep test to check brain activity and then let's throw in an ultra sound just to check her chest area.

First stop - CAT scan. We arrive early because we weren't sure as to where to go, but we found it without incident. Mom is checked in, we are the only ones in the waiting area so we know we are first, Mom is in a good mood, great, no problem . . . no problem? Why do I assume stuff like that?

Ten minute wait becomes half an hour, the waiting room is filling up. Mom is getting quiet and I am praying she's quiet because she's just nervous about going in. Nope. Mom is taking in all of the "conversations" around her and now she feels the need to share.

Mom – "Wow, look at all these black people here."
Me – "Mom, please, there are lots of people here for the same test as you are, you will be going in shortly."
Mom – "Have you ever noticed that when one of them come in for a test, they bring pretty much their whole family?"
Me – . . . dumbfounded, and whispering "Mom, please, let's just be quiet a minute and wait for our turn."
Mom – . . . louder than before "No really and they do all that religious and preaching stuff, why is it black people do that?"

Everyone turns and looks at me wondering why I can't control her.

Me – "Mom, we need to be quiet before your test or they won't be able to do an accurate reading of your brain to see what's wrong and why you aren't thinking right." Pretty cleaver on my part I'm thinking.
Mom – . . . silent, thinking for a minute, "My brain is fine, don't you wonder?". . . and I hear the nurse call her name, thank goodness. In she goes, and I head off to the other waiting room where I am not being eyed like some villain.

So the rest of the day goes smoothly, each test is done quickly and we are out the door by supper time with no added incidents today. Whew.

9.   Eye Doctor time — here's some humor

So here we are for an easy eye apt, first apt of the day, Mom hasn't had any issues since having her cataract surgery so this should be a quick routine check and we should be on our way.

Normal eye exam, eye drops in for dilation and off to the waiting room while her eyes dilate, normal stuff, easy and she's pretty quiet so far. Nurse calls us in and does the standard look at the wall, cover one eye stuff and everything is good, she currently uses glasses just when she drives every now and then (yes, she still drives –more stories on that later) and now comes the fun.

Nurse - Hands my mom a card "Norma, without your glasses can you read the card I just gave you?"
Mom - "Of course, but I'm sure you've read it, don't you know what it says already?"
Me - . . . thinking, oh great, here we go. . .
Nurse - . . . grinning"Yes, I do, but I need you to read it for me."
Mom - Silent.
Nurse - "Can you read that Norma?"
Mom - "Yes, I just read it."
Nurse - "I need you to read that out loud please."
Mom - "Well, you didn't say that (to which I have to admit she didn't tell her to read it out loud).

Nurse - . . .smiling, "No I guess I didn't say that, so can you just to this for me, can you just read the smallest line on that card for me, out loud?"

Ready for this . . .?

Mom - "Copyright 1988 vision company, etc." (very bottom of the card in extremely small print.)
Nurse - "Excuse me, I'm sorry can you read that again?"
Mom - Repeats: "Copyright 1988 vision company, etc."
Me - . . . laughing out loud "You did tell her to read the smallest line on the card."
Nurse - "Yes I did, and Norma? I don't think you need those glasses anymore."

Doctor comes in, we all have a good laugh to which they both say they have never had anyone do that before (because they haven't met my Mom!) and they both agree glasses aren't needed any longer. Not bad for an 82 yr old woman.

So in a sense with dementia it's like talking to a child at times, be very precise on what you ask for because believe it or not, they are listening to every detail as this shows.

Section Two – Okay things aren't so humorous anymore. . .

1.   Picture albums

One of the best "projects" I did with my Mom towards the end was making photo albums. She was staring at her bookcase filled with about a dozen photo albums one day and said to me "Boy are you going to have fun going through all these photo albums when I'm gone Bethie" to which I replied "Hell no, we are going to do it now while you're here to help me" . . . and we both laughed and agreed that yeah, maybe this would be cool to do together, so off to the hobby store we went.

There are 4 of us kids so to start we bought 4 photo albums, glue sticks, paper and everything needed to make some cool books that hopefully my brothers will cherish as much as I know I'm going to. Each book starts with birth pictures and ends with the most current pictures, this included all the family gatherings, school photos, girlfriends/boyfriends, weddings, grandchildren, all of it. We did this in her living room for almost two months, she on the couch telling me who should get what picture and me on the floor with books, glue sticks and pictures scattered everywhere.

We talked about people we hadn't seen in years, memories of things we have all gone through and at times laughed so hard we were in tears. Being the youngest I had an amazing history lesson daily on my ancestors and even learned things about my own father I never knew, like when I saw a picture of him next to a race car and I asked where that was taken and she said "Oh, that's when your dad had the race car we use to race." Umm, what? How cool is that? Then there were other times that she would look at pictures, get that blank almost scared look on her face and tell me she didn't know who those people were in the pictures to which I knew at that time we needed to take a break and focus on what and who she knew at that time and get her mind off the overwhelming feeling of losing control of her memories. It's awful to see your 83 yr old mother look at a picture of your brothers, tears in her eyes, look me square in the eye and say "I don't know who these people are." To which my first thought is how scared I am right now and how much I want to cry because my mom is slipping away right in front of me, but I pulled it together, sat on the couch next to her and said "Oh, those are just my stupid brothers," hugged her and said "Yeah, I'm trying to forget who they are too, so we're doing just fine Mom." And, to that she smiled and actually started laughing, "Yeah," she said, "we're doing fine."

This project took us a good two to three months and at Christmas that year she gave each of my siblings their book. Everyone was amazed and one of my "stupid" brothers was actually in tears.

What an amazing gift I was given to be able to do this with my Mom before things got too bad. That was the last Christmas we had with her and I will forever be grateful for the laughs and tears while working on this "project" with her.

2.   Dementia

So as you are told your parent has dementia your first thought is panic, what am I going to do? How bad is this? What happens next? Can they live on their own? I wanted to scream and or cry all at the same time. Do I tell Mom? How will this impact her life if I do? All the while I just wanted to bust out crying, run to my Mom and tell her so she could make it all better, but wait, I can't, it's her that this is affecting so that isn't an option. The child in me is horrified. So I need to pull myself together, educate myself the best I can, ask questions and be ready for what is next.

I was so fortunate to have such an amazing doctor that put it all on the line for me, flat out bold and honest as to what I was going to be dealing with and how hard it was going to be to handle. He told me what to look for, how it would affect her and how her anger would be geared towards me since I was the closest one to her. He said once it truly kicked in that she was going to deteriorate quickly because of the type of dementia we were dealing with. So with their added support at the doctor's office to be there for questions and appointments at any time, I felt I had the support to help me with any decisions I needed to make on this scary, bumpy unknown road I was about to venture forth with; and, for my Mom having the utmost respect for her independence and privacy as I would want for myself if this was handed to me in later life.

I made the decision to not tell my Mom right away that dementia was on the table, I wanted her to maintain her lifestyle independently as long as she possibly could all the while keeping closer tabs on her more than ever before. I didn't tell any of her friends or her neighbors because it really is a life changing thing and at first with very few signs of something "different" about her out there, I didn't want anyone treating her differently or talking about it. I guess I went into protective mode.

The first two years were pretty uneventful but once things started happening with her memory and she was realizing something wasn't quite right and getting a bit scared at times I knew it was time to tell her. So we sat down one afternoon and discussed exactly what was happening and why, all the while trying my hardest not to scare her more than she was and not letting on how scared I was inside at the thought of losing my Mom.

She was a bit upset at first and had lots of questions (which thank goodness from doing some pretty extensive research I was ready for all her questions) we decided together not to tell anyone else right now, that we would deal with things as they came up and go from there. The most important thing is she knew she was not alone, that we were in this together and her knowing that gave her the strength and trust in me to handle anything we had coming at us.

Through all of this scary stuff one conversation we had still makes me laugh to this day. We had just come home from a doctor's apt for her that lasted most of the day and she was asking me all kinds of stuff. I remember being so exhausted from the day's events with my patience wearing thin I answered her with a quick "I don't know, I can't remember right now Mom" to which she stopped me, looked me square in the eye and said "Huh, and I'm the one with dementia." I just burst out laughing and we both laughed until we had tears. That was my real Mom coming through, loud and clear.

3.   The "Monster" surfaces

Well, my term for dementia is flat out "Monster." This is the best way I can describe something that has taken someone you love and turned them into something else unwillingly. A Monster.

My Mom was living in a retirement apartment village for roughly 4 months, was adjusting well and seemed to be happy in her new surroundings. Now mind you she wasn't really happy to move out of her house that she lived in for 50+ years, but knew that it was time that she not have the worry of stairs or maintaining a home anymore; this was a time for her to relax and be around people her own age that share the same interests she has at this time in her life so she was happy to be somewhere very safe and comfortable. She also had a lifelong friend that had an apartment down the hall and was starting to mingle with other people for brunches and things like that so things were looking good . . .until she got sick.

I stopped to see her as I normally do each night and this particular night she was having a awful time breathing, so off to the hospital we go for a breathing treatment. She has half a lung on the left side due to surgery in 2001 to remove a suspicious mass and has done pretty well up until the last few years when we have had more trips to the hospital when breathing got difficult. This would normally consist of a breathing treatment and she would feel much better and we would head on home, but not this trip.

Mom goes in and we have 2 breathing treatments this time and things just aren't going as well as they normally do, she still is very short of breath and the decision is made for her to stay overnight about which she is very angry with me now for bringing her in, pretty normal for her, I mean really, who wants to stay in the hospital anyways, so I understand.

Mom spends three days in the hospital where her confusion worsens, she is angry at night to the point that one night she was medicated and restrained, to which I learn a new term the "Monster" brings with it: Sundowners. Sundowners is a condition where people with Alzheimer's and/or dementia get more agitated as the day falls into night, nothing they can really do except medicate them to calm them down. It's horrible.

Mom is released after three days, is sent home with an oxygen tank full time now because we have also learned that she has emphysema and is battling a bit of pneumonia. We get her settled in, she is resting and the next day at lunch time I go to make sure she is eating and she looks at me and says, "I think I came home too soon." She can't catch her breath and we call an ambulance to take her to the hospital.

Mom spends the next entire week in the hospital with breathing treatments each day, meds for pneumonia and her confusion is worsening, I am there first thing in the morning, lunch time and right after work until she falls asleep and many times was called back up because she is yelling for me and I absolutely do not want her to be restrained ever again.

It's horrible to watch one of the strongest people you know in the world be in such fear of something that isn't true. My Mom had one night of pure panic and horror because she was convinced the nurses were trying to kill her in the hospital. I watched in pure angst as just she and I were in her hospital room as tears flowed down her face because she was so scared as I did all I could to convince her it wasn't true. I snuggled up next to her bed and held her hand to reassure her I would stay and protect her and from then on I stayed every night with her to make sure she was not only comfortable but felt safe in her surroundings to help fend off what the "Monster" was dealing her that night because in her mind, it was real.

One of the hardest parts of this awful dementia is that at times Mom didn't know who I was, she at times thought I was her mother (a term of endearment as a caregiver I learned) and other times would look me square in the eye and tell me she didn't know me. Those days were the worst because inside to myself I was screaming, "Mom it's me! How can you not know your own daughter?" It was awful, it kind of felt like she didn't love me anymore because I was just some stranger staring at her and she could care less, but the days she did know me? Were absolute gifts and those were the days I didn't want her to go to sleep because I wanted so desperately to hang on to my Mom, the real Mom I knew for what brief time I had with her that day.

4.   Release from the hospital

So here comes another tough decision, what to do now that she's too healthy to stay in the hospital but too sick to go home . . . Rehab. Rehab in a nursing facility with full care to help her hopefully get back on her feet and independent again at least that is the goal, I wasn't ready to give up on that yet. Although the "Monster" had other plans.

So when you are faced with something like this all of a sudden you are told you have a "case worker for your situation" (what a cold way to explain your loved one's exit from the hospital, now my Mom is a situation? No, I don't think so). Anyways, you're handed a list of possible nursing home facilities and we all know no one wants to be in a nursing home and for me especially I didn't want to place my Mom in just any facility if I could help it. So down the list I go, thankfully one of my closest friends has an aunt in a facility and she can't praise it enough so this will be my first stop.

Side note: when you get to the point of picking out a place to have your loved one the best advice I can give is to picture yourself there and ask yourself, is this somewhere I would want to be and feel comfortable? This is exactly what I did and the first stop I made was the only place I visited and it was the best choice I honestly could have made for my Mom and still feel that way today after all that has happened.

5.   Hardest month and a half of my life

-April 11, 2014

Time for Mom to be released from the hospital. She wants to go home of course, but she also understands that with her health the way it is right now that she can't go home like this and take care of herself, so a Rehab facility is the plan for the next 100 days, she's ok with that.

The place I chose was a long term care facility that offers everything she needed. She had her own private room, full on nursing care 24 hrs a day and rehab during the day to help get her back on her feet and hopefully home soon to live independently once again.

We arrange to get her to the facility and the first one to greet her is the Activity Director and they hit it off right away. I get there shortly after (since she had to go in by Ambu-care) to help Mom settle in and she is nowhere to be found. Here I thought she would be in her room miserable and she is already off with the Activity Director eating ice cream with the other residents, something my Mom would normally never do, but I take this as a good sign that she is feeling comfortable in her new surroundings already so this is great.

Mom spends the next couple of weeks working with physical therapy, speech therapy, occupational therapy and trying like heck to get feeling better until she is hit with another bout of pneumonia and an added Urinary Tract Infection (UTI), to which if you aren't familiar with UTI's, they can really mess up elderly people, confusion, anger and a lot of sleeping accompany these nasty infections, a total transformation of personalities is more like it. We get thru both of these infections and things are looking better again, so back on track with therapy until pneumonia hits again, another setback, but being the trouper Mom is she beats this bout too and things are looking much better.

-May 1st

Birthday time. Mom's birthday is May 1st, so I have decided that with all the people helping with her care that I would get her a half a sheet cake and cookies to celebrate with everyone at her facility to thank them for everything they are doing and have done for her, this will be fun.

I stayed late the night before and decorated her room after she fell asleep so when she woke up the first things she would see were all about her birthday, so everyone knew it was a special day, her special day and we were going to be up later that night with cake to celebrate it right!

We were so fortunate that Mom was where she was at, the Activity Director arranges parties for all of the residents on their birthdays so they all feel special, now mind you there are a lot of residents that don't have family members that visit them so Activity Director makes their day special no matter what. I told the staff we were going to have cake so they had ice cream sundaes for Mom in the afternoon to celebrate, lots of pictures were taken and Mom had a blast. It was "her day". I got there shortly after 5 as I normally do loaded up with treats for everyone to have after dinner was served and what did my mom do? She fell asleep and could hardly eat her b-day cake! She had such an incredible fun and busy day that she was totally wiped out.

Mom turned 84 that day, this was her last birthday with us and the Activity Director made sure she was not only remembered, but made it so it wasn't just another day, for which I will always be grateful.

-May 2nd

I got to the care facility shortly after 5 like normal to be greeted by Mom's favorite nurse aide with a horrified look on her face and asked me if I talked to the nurse yet. "No, why?" She couldn't tell me so I hurried towards Mom's room to be stopped by the nurse and doctor telling me Mom had been overdosed on one of her meds, her heart medication, so an ambulance was called. I get into Mom's room where when she sees me she starts to cry and I see the panic in her eyes, I crawl into bed with her and calm her down as best I can under the circumstances when all I really want to do is tear apart the staff that has done this to her but I obviously know that will not do me any good so remaining calm and trying to get as much information as I can right now is key to what will happen going forward.

Mom is calm by the time the ambulance arrives and she understands that we are going to the hospital for just observation and have some blood work done just to make sure she is alright, Mom is okay with this because I told her I would stay there with her until she is brought back to her room here at the care facility, no overnight stays alone in the hospital ever again for her.

Mom was taken to the E. R. for observation to make sure if she had any side effects from the overdose she was in the best place possible. This is a very scary thing to have happen to her when she has a DNR (Do Not Resuscitate) on file, so if she has any side effects that stop her heart there is nothing they will do to bring her back.

The E.R. doctor on that night is Dr. Boyer, one of the most amazing doctors I have ever met which you will understand why I say that a bit later. Dr. Boyer comes in, explains that blood work needs to be done as well as an EKG for the monitoring of her heart while she is there along with contacting Poison Control to not only report what has happened but the hospital needed to follow their guidelines. So Mom is hooked up to monitors, drinking lots of water to help with flushing out her system and is nice and calm.

Everything seems ok to us from the extra heart med we were told she was given. Dr. Boyer comes in and explains we can leave as soon as the results come back from the 3rd med she was overdosed on. Wait, what? 3rd med? We were told 1 med, did you say 3 meds? Yes, the doctor said, 3. Turns out Mom was overdosed on heart, blood thinner and blood pressure meds. Not a good combination for an 84 yr old woman with an irregular heartbeat to start with. We both looked at each other and knew at that exact moment how lucky we were.

Mom spent roughly 4 hrs in E.R. that night, she came through with no side effects whatsoever and with the dementia I figured she probably wouldn't remember much about what happened in the morning, but then again we never truly know how the brain works especially when there is a "Monster" lurking within do we?

Mom spent most of the next day sleeping, drinking lots of water to help finish flushing out the extra meds that were in her system and no meds were given that day; she just needed lots of rest. Everyone at the care facility was on edge wondering what was going to happen next, were we going to press charges, did we have to move her, what would happen to the nurses involved, lots of uncertainty. My biggest concern of course was still Mom, her care, and was she still comfortable there? So after talking with her we made the decision to have her stay put. She loved all her caregivers, felt safe and comfortable and that was the most important thing for me that she felt safe and comfortable. We chalked this up to a mistake, people are human and mistakes are made. And when you really think about it, her level of care and concern from the staff was definitely going to be increased because everyone was going to be extra cautious with her now.

Sunday morning. We are now two days after the incident and I'm thinking she is awake, things are seeming back to normal and with this dementia she isn't going to remember anything that happened, so I'm not going to mention it and just as we are sitting on her bed reading the paper one of my friends came in for a visit and she said "Wow Norma, you look great!" My Mom looks at me, smiles and said back to her, "yeah, can you believe they overdosed me? I spent almost 4 hrs in the emergency room when we thought it was 1 medication only to find out it was 3". I just started laughing and thought, yep, today is going to be a good day, Mom, my real Mom is coming through loud and clear. Take that "Monster lurking within."

Dementia is a very mean thing at times, it can take this person you love so much who would never ever think of hurting you into someone you don't really know anymore because of the things they say to you looking you square in the eye. I watched for almost 6 yrs as my Mom slowly deteriorated in front of me. I saw all the highs and all the lows that the "Monster" handed us.

I saw my strong willed fiercely independent Mom turn into an unsure, scared, angry and confused woman. I had days where she didn't have a clue who I was but didn't want me to leave because for some reason I was someone familiar to her and she felt safe and more comfortable with me just staying there with her. Then we had days where she would introduce me to the staff that has been caring for her for the last month because today she knew who I was and was so happy I was there, to which we all played along because this was a great day for Mom.

-Missing her parents and sister

During the course of the month of May my Mom had very vivid dreams of her Mom and Dad and was calling out for her sister. The more she talked about them the more I knew she missed them. She said she really wanted to talk to her Daddy, broke my heart because although I understood what she was saying, it meant she was going to have to leave me to have that happen. Mom told me numerous times she was ready to go and I remember asking her point blank "You don't want to hang out here with me anymore?" I'm a lot of fun ya know. . ." kind of laughing it off as we normally do with serious things to lighten it up. And, she just looked at me ever so serious and said "no." I told her "If you leave me then I won't see you for a long time" to which she said nothing and just looked at me as if she was hoping I would understand what she was saying to me, and I did.

We had a couple very hard discussions in regards to her being ready to go and not worrying about me anymore, one night was extremely hard as she was in bed with me leaning over her when she grabbed the collar of my shirt in the front of my chest and said "Bethie, I'm worried about you" and I said "Why? You don't need to worry about me Mom," then she said if "I don't worry about you who will?" After going back and forth on this about 3 times I finally said, "How about we leave that up to Matt?" (my son), to which she seemed pretty content with that answer and she simply drifted off to sleep.

Shortly after that we had another discussion about how ready she was to go, how she wakes up each morning and says to herself, "I'm still here, guess I have to do this again." How she missed her family and after hearing how deep in her heart I knew she meant this we talked about, yeah, if you're that ready then you need to stop worrying about what's going on here, let all of that go and get the rest you need to visit them all in Heaven. And again I knew she wasn't feeling well and at this point who was she fighting for? Me, because she was worried about me?

I reassured her that all would be fine if she was that ready, no more worries about anything. . . that it wouldn't be easy by any means for me, but she knew how much I loved her and I needed to make it easy for her, let her know that if she wanted to stop the fight and go to the next phase of her journey it was ok, her quality of life wasn't anything near what she would have wanted and she was tired, so very tired, it was time for her to rest. I told her each and every day that I loved her, so she knew clearly how I felt about her. The child in me didn't want to lose her Mom, but the grown up in me knew exactly what she was telling me.

6.   The end is near

Mom was in the Care Facility for the next 27 days, we had our ups and downs of not feeling well and sleeping all day to feeling great and walking all over the facility with her walker. The weekend of May 24th was one of the best weekends my Mom had at the Care Facility.

Saturday was pretty normal for us, some walking, a nice dinner; Mom seemed really calm and clear. We had a really good conversation that day, it was nice to have her back to talk to.

Sunday I went up as I normally do and we normally would read the paper on her bed and watch black and white movies and usually have a visit from at least someone. On this particular day she was feeling really good. I got there to find her sitting up in her recliner waiting for me to help get her new favorite purple sneakers on so we could walk and walking we did! No oxygen on (off for almost a week now) and she grabbed her walker and up and down the whole facility we went, we walked from one end to the other only stopping to see the birds in the Aviary like we do daily (normally in a wheelchair after dinner), but this time we actually sat in the lobby and talked for a bit. Another great day.

-Monday, May 26th

Monday seemed pretty normal, Mom worked with all her therapists and was feeling good. A bit of confusion has kicked in and she just doesn't seem like her normal self, I figured she was probably just tired from the great weekend she had and all the therapy today. Get her meds and breathing treatment done and once she is ready for bed she is out like a light, no worries, and straight to sleep before her head hits the pillow.

-Tuesday May 27th

Mom just isn't feeling good, doesn't really want to eat and confusion is worsening so I'm not forcing anything, something isn't quite right so I ask for a UTI test and sure enough she has another infection so meds are started for that. She is tired and she pretty much just wants to watch some TV. She picks at her food and is nodding off, so we get her evening meds done, breathing treatment and off to bed she goes. She is sleeping about half an hour and she wakes up looking confused, her breathing isn't good and she just can't calm down, so I crawl in bed with her reassure her everything is alright and she just needs to get some rest, all the while I'm thinking her breathing isn't sounding good at all, but eventually she does fall asleep and has a somewhat restful night.

-Wednesday May 28th and the "Monster" takes over

When I get there to see Mom she is a bit restless, not wanting to eat dinner and more confusion has set in. We agree she should try to eat something because she's probably just tired from the busy day. She eats a little and is just not feeling right, nurses come in and check her oxygen levels and they aren't good so the oxygen is put back on and a chest x-ray is ordered before she goes to bed. Chest x-ray is done and yes, she has pneumonia again, meds are started immediately. We get her other nightly meds and breathing treatment done and she is off to bed. She is just not getting comfortable so as our routine is getting I crawl in bed with her, try to diminish any fears she has that is not letting her rest and she wants to talk about her Mother and Daddy, she has been constantly talking about her sister that died 24 years earlier and how she is having dreams about them, she misses them. Yes, I know the end is coming, she's ready, trying to get me ready, but I'm hoping not too soon.

-Thursday May 29th

I get there right after 5:00 to find Mom in her recliner having a breathing treatment. I'm told an ambulance has been called because of her oxygen levels being so low and with the newly added pneumonia they just wanted to be safe and have her monitored closer at the hospital. So I explained all of this to Mom who was in a bit of a panic because of her last hospital visit, but I promise her I will be with her the entire time and if she has to stay the night that I will stay the night, if she is there for days, I will stay for days. I will stay until she comes back to the Care Facility. As I'm looking at her all I can think is this is different, this time her breathing, her color and how she is acting is different. We have had many breathing issues, but this one, this is different, so off to the hospital we go.

We meet in the E.R. about 15 minutes later to find that Dr. Boyer is on tonight and all I can think is thank God because I know she is thorough and great with Mom so we will get an answer to what is happening and get her back to her room at the care facility in no time. Mom has a breathing treatment, an EKG, blood work is started and a chest x-ray is next. Mom still is having a hard time breathing so another breathing treatment is started, now mind you, she has had 4 breathing treatments in less than 2 hrs.

I'm standing next to Mom's bed when Dr. Boyer pops back in and asks Mom about her breathing, what hurts, etc. Then she starts to quietly ask me under the noise of the machine hooked up to Mom administering her breathing treatments "What are your Mom's final wishes? Has she indicated that she is ready to go?"

This I was not prepared for at this moment, yes I knew what she wanted, but this was supposed to be an easy, "Let's get a breathing treatment, catch our breath and go back to her room so she can rest." I knew she was dreaming about her parents and calling out to her sister and at times telling me she was ready, but at this exact moment, no, no, I wasn't ready, no, not yet. So as I watch them start the 5th breathing treatment Dr. Boyer said her x-rays are back and asked me what I decided for her further measures to which the child in me wanted to run to my Mom for comfort and make it all go away but the grown up in me said I need to pull it together and help my Mom deal with what is coming.

Dr. Boyer and I step outside to where she explains how she remembers Mom and knows all her health conditions from her last trip here and how there are so many factors battling against her at this point and continues to tell me exactly what is going on and what can be done as far as cleaning out her lungs which would be horrible and how it's time to let go. She gave me an example of how wonderful medicine is to prolong life but when things are like they are with Mom and how tired she is of the fight each time she comes here, who is she fighting for? Is it fair to have her continue a fight she, her body just can't endure any longer?

As she is talking she said "It's kind of like in the old days before all this medicine came about, this is when you would rally the troops and let them go peacefully." No! I'm screaming in my head, it's not that easy.

So I'm standing there point blank with Dr. Boyer and she said, "It's time to let her go." (No I'm screaming in my head.) When I asked "How do I make that decision? If I say, "yeah, it's time, make her comfortable," is it because I'm tired of all this after 6 yrs of nonstop care and want to quit because I'm tired and selfish or is it the right decision for Mom? She said "It's the right decision for Mom, let her go peacefully and gracefully." I just started crying, this is not the way tonight was supposed to go, not even close.

So she told me we would look at the x-rays together and if it's what she suspects, then it's a blessing from God helping me make the decision.

So we walk in, half lung on the left is clear, full lung on the right has pneumonia right in the middle; she said it was like Mom is breathing through a sponge. I was stunned, didn't know what to think and was flat out numb. We talked a bit more and it was decided Hospice would be the best place to have Mom go. Dr. Boyer said she would call the Hospice facility and see what beds were available. She didn't put this call off on someone, she made the call herself, she knew I was struggling and was really trying her best to help me.

We went back in with Mom and she explained to Mom that she understood that she had been talking about her parents which indicated she was ready to go.

I will never forget the panicked look in my Mom's eyes when she realized the decision had been made (I live with that awful image to this day) as Dr. Boyer started explaining what would be done to keep her comfortable and I said to my Mom "Mom, I think you have been trying to get me ready for about a month now" to which she shook her head "yes."

Mom was taken off all her machines, breathing treatments finished first dose of morphine in and I hugged her, told her I loved her twice to which she said "I love you too Bethie" she wrapped her left arm around me and gently patted me on the back like all caring mothers do to try to calm down a hurting child.

My Mom went to sleep shortly after that and never fully woke up. I have her last words, as selfish as that seems having 3 brothers, I have her last words.

For 6 years with the first mention of Dementia I watched over her, stood by her side during hard and scary Dr.'s appointments, cared for her when things got difficult. And when things got out of control to the point I could not help her physically I made sure she was in the best possible place to be. We made decisions together up until she no longer could and I hope and pray to this day I made decisions for her she would be happy with and be proud of me for following her last wishes.

Mom died 19 hrs later in the most amazing Hospice Residence our hometown has to offer. She left this world knowing I was at her side, I truly loved her and the room was filled with love.

Mom, you were my rock.
I miss you terribly.
I love you. . .
Bethie

7.   Guilt

As a caregiver one of the hardest things I know of is the guilt I felt knowing I couldn't personally give my Mom the care that she needed, I wasn't trained or had enough medical knowledge to help her the way she was going to need it. In a way that is the hardest thing to admit and the best thing to admit because it showed that I understood the severity of what she was facing and I wanted to get her the best care possible I could.

For the last 6 years of my Mom's life I had contact with her every day. As the dementia progressed I actually saw her every other day physically and numerous calls the other days until it progressed to the point of her needing me to see her every night. I was always just a phone call away and was at her house in a matter of minutes whenever I heard that certain tone in her voice that told me something wasn't quite right, hard to explain but once you're in the midst of something like this you understand.

8. The car and the house

The decision to have Mom move out of her house into an apartment wasn't easy. Mom was a very independent woman her whole life and never once asked anyone for anything.

She remained home and driving up until she had her second car accident, this will come as a surprise to my brothers as they read this because we (Mom and I) decided that telling them would only bring embarrassment to her and she did not want to upset them. The first accident was when a young girl hit her and convinced my Mom the damage was minimal and with Mom's confusion she believed her and the girl drove off leaving Mom with a very dented up car. Mom felt awful telling me and thought I would take her driving privileges away to which when I calmed her down and explained it wasn't her fault she felt much better. Once again she knew by telling me we would figure it out without having her feel worse than she already did.

The second accident was a simple thing where she backed into someone and it was an honest accident. That night when I got there to see her she actually handed me her car keys and said she didn't want to drive anymore, she was afraid my oldest brother would yell at her and she was scared.

We had a long talk that night and it was decided that the last thing I wanted to do was take her independence away with everything else that was coming ahead with the dementia, she understood that maybe just quick trips to the store would be alright, but all the other places she needed to go would be a joint venture with me, no one knew our agreement, no one questioned that her driving was getting less and less and once again she wasn't "different", dementia hadn't won yet.

The exact moment when the move from the house was decided was very difficult. Mom was thinking it was a good idea then backed off for about six months. I didn't push her I simply spent more time with her and as things progressed she made the decision to move on her own.

It came down to two different instances where she went out to some free food trucks (yes, she went early in the morning and got free food and distributed it to the neighbors that weren't working in the neighborhood that were too proud to go, something not many people knew about my Mom). Anyways, the last two times that she went by the time she got home she couldn't remember what day it was, she seemed to lose a day or two in there and the panic in her was awful. It took me a good solid two to three hours each time to get her back on board with what day it was and that she didn't lose any time anywhere, the panic is indescribable and to hear it in her voice would get me to her house in minutes because I knew she was terrified.

So as everyone around us thought I was a pushy daughter to get her to move and listening to all the people that said "How could I do this to my Mom who lived there for so many years?" I remained silent and took all the crap talk they wanted to give, give it to me and leave Mom alone. They didn't realize what was truly going on in that house that I was in and out of all hours of the night and day helping Mom fight off whatever dementia was offering that day. As long as Mom was safe and didn't have to listen to anyone around her talk about her being sick or "different" I was good. Another "protective" mode.

Once Mom was moved into her apartment our routine changed to my going there every night after work to and pretty much spending the weekends with her. So if I spent so much time with her, why do I feel guilty? I think the guilt comes from the wishing I could have done more.

Even after she moved into the care facility, every night we had a routine of dinner, nightly meds, her and I doing her breathing treatments so once she was in bed I would either sit beside her rubbing her arm until she fell asleep or if the "Monster" surfaced with something that scared her I would sit right in bed with her reassuring her everything was alright until she fell asleep. The people closest to me that were there on occasion and witnessed this say they don't understand how I could feel one ounce of guilt. To me, even to this day I don't think I did enough. There is still the feeling I could have done more. What that is? I don't have an answer, but I'm still beating myself up about it.

9.   A stranger's "thank you"

It didn't dawn on me until almost 5 months after Mom passed away and revisiting almost daily the final two days with her and how horrible it was that I received a thank you from a total stranger for making that awful decision that night to help her end her pain and suffering in the way we did with dignity.

As were waiting for the transit ride for Mom from the hospital to the Hospice facility the ambulance driver that brought her in popped his head in and asked how things were, I was such a mess I just shook my head 'no' to which he replied, "I'm sorry for your loss, but thank you for being 'that person'. . . "That person"? "That strong person to say, yes it's time" I just remember looking at him and thinking "sorry for my loss" not dawning on me the full extent of what he meant until now.

I remember getting up and walking outside the room to talk to him and he said he remembers bringing my Mom in once before and all her breathing conditions concerned him with her quality of life. He explained to me that he knew it wasn't an easy decision, but I needed to understand it was the right decision.

He then shared a story with me of a woman he transports periodically between the nursing home and hospital when she is sick that is on a feeding tube that is unable to speak or walk that has not only no quality of life, but no family that will step up to help her make decisions based on her care, so that poor woman is in a state of ongoing suffering with no one to help, how in a sense she is trapped. I remember feeling awful for this woman and wondering how that happens and how many people are out there suffering like that?

That is one thing my Mom made clear to me, she was ready, she had the DNR in place for a reason and that she had me as her medical advocate to make this decision when it was time. So as awful as it was to "step up" and abide by her wishes. I am grateful she had everything in place to help me.

Section Three - Little things: Time to share some hopefully helpful tips in caring

Ok, so these are some of the weird things I did when caring for my Mom that as I have told her story people have said, "Hey, that's a really cool idea", so here goes . . .

1.   Animals are amazing

Enter Rowdy. So in my research of people and the effects of dementia and the thinking process I learned that one of the best things for them is a pet, something they can concentrate on and drown out the everyday things that may get them worried. So if there is not a pet in the home it's worth considering for sure as I did with Rowdy (I still feel bad to this day that I lied to her about how I got Rowdy) the truth is I adopted the beautiful two month old kitten that fit in the palm of your hand, very independent from all the others in the cage at a pet facility because I thought she would be perfect for my very independent Mom, a perfect match in my eyes. Now I have to get Mom on board with having a new kitten.

Mom has had cats all her life and when her buddy "George" passed away at 16 it hurt her so bad that she swore she would never have another one, so I needed to get creative. I told Mom that I found this poor little kitten in the bushes down by the foundry downtown and apparently she is fixed already and asked would she want another kitten, flat out *NO!*. Great . . . now what am I going to do with this poor little thing?

So I physically brought her over to see her and asked her to think on it again to which she replied "Ok, we can try it." I promised her I would take care of the litter, feeding, etc. to which she agreed sounded good, long story short, this little cat was more in tune with her than most people. They absolutely fell in love with each other and was one of the best things I could have given her at that time, she just doted on Rowdy and would laugh when she did silly things and it gave her something to concentrate on besides her world of confusion and worry that was sinking in quickly.

There is one thing that strikes me still when I think of it to this day involving interaction between my Mom and Rowdy. One evening when I stopped at my Mom's after work I found her having a very confusing day and as I came in the door Rowdy came by me playing like crazy and just in the instant my Mom started talking and things weren't making much sense, Rowdy stopped in her tracks, crawled up on the arm of the chair next to my Mom and laid there still as could be until Mom started talking clearly again. It was like she sensed something was wrong and knew everything needed to be calm. I watched this in awe as they connected and tell people about this all the time. I've never witnessed anything like this before. Animals are amazing creatures, there is a lot we can learn from them if we just take the time to stop, watch and listen.

Calmness, an amazing peacefulness will follow if received properly.

I have Rowdy now and she is a blessing to me as a reminder of my Mom and one of the last things she truly loved.

2.   Reminders

Calendar for appointments. Dementia definitely changes the thought process. I found as my Mom progressed if you told her something that needed to be done in the future she would obsess about it and remind me every day for fear of herself that she would forget so we had a large desk calendar on her kitchen table. As I scheduled appointments I would mark this on the calendar and we were in agreement that we wouldn't worry about things until that month in which we were dealing. This gave her the control to know what was happening and when and she could make notes as well, so it calmed her thought process down. I also had all her appointments in my phone calendar so when she would get confused and call me I could pull it up and we could figure it out immediately with no added worries, she knew I was on top of it, problem solved.

3.   **The calm of laundry detergent**

So Mom is in a care facility and they have a full on laundry dept that will come in and wash everything the residents have that they want washed which is great, some residents don't have family come in so they have no worry that their clothes and such will be cleaned, but Mom was stuck with me going there every day so I will do her laundry, my choice.

Why did I do this? I did this for Mom, when she was home doing her own laundry and as it slowly got to me just doing it for her once a week I noticed that when she was in the hospital she was restless at night and it dawned on me that maybe, just maybe as she fell asleep, there wasn't that smell of home, her laundry detergent, something I guess I would call calming, something I could control over the dementia to be familiar at least.

So when I was asked why I did her laundry? It was because even though she was in this beautiful comfortable amazing facility, it still wasn't home and if I could bring her just a piece of that as she snuggled up at night to rest, then that's what I tried to do.

4.   The Day

So as dementia kicks in there are things that are really scary for people that have it. One thing is what day is it? Not so much the date, but what day of the week is it and if you don't have something solid to show them to reassure them, they won't believe you. Sure the newspaper is a good source, but that also turns into them being unsure because they aren't sure if they picked it up yesterday or today because they can't remember what happened yesterday which made for even more confused scary situations for Mom, so I got her a clock, big bold letters with the actual day on it --Mon, Tues, Wed, etc.; well that was great until the power went out and it was reset time and she couldn't remember what day to reset it to -- that was a mess.

So it dawned on me one day. . .

Cell phone! She has a cell phone! So we decided when that confusion kicks in and you feel scared because you lost a day, pop open that cell phone and there it is bold as ever -- the day! We never had a day where it was a question ever again, she was good!

Oh and as a side note here, Mom and I were in a gas station one day and an older gentleman picked up a newspaper and proceeded to argue with the attendant about them having the wrong papers out on the stand because it was the following day to which my Mom looked at me, grinned and walked over to the gentleman and after a brief conversation he pulled out his cell phone, looked around, apologized to the attendant hugged my Mom and walked out. She came back proud as could be that she helped him and all I thought was something so scary to her until we resolved it recently was a tool she used to reach out to someone in her same scared confused community, it was amazing to watch, she was in control still and she knew it.

5. New items

Some of the simplest things to you and I are almost like the end of the world to the person dementia is affecting. Introducing them to something new/cool/fun for us is simply scary to them.

For instance, a coffee maker. Making a pot of coffee as they have done for years is easy, leave it alone. Nope -- someone thought a fancy new "easier" single cup coffee maker would be better. So again, what is easier to you is a nightmare to them. They will use it the best that they can to not hurt your feelings, but the caregiver is actually the one explaining how to use it to them daily.

So when something like this happens easy notes or instructions came into play with us. And this is how it works with Dementia:

First day it's great, it's fun, it's new and exciting.

Day two, how do I turn it on?
How do I make a cup of coffee with it?
We go thru all the details again, no problem.

Day three, repeat of day two. How do I turn it on, how do I make coffee with it?

Yes you see the pattern, so how did we make it easier for her so she wasn't embarrassed if people stopped over? Simple notes and I mean simple:

1. Turn the power button on.
2. Insert coffee k-cup.
3. Press Brew.

Yes, before this simple 3 item list this new machine was earth shatteringly scary because it was one more thing she was losing control over. So even though I didn't mind making lists (we got really good at it actually) the best advice I have is to not change up too many "familiar things" it only scares them more.

Same thing for the TV remote and channels. A simple list on how to turn her TV on and off with the remote. And when she couldn't remember when her favorite shows were on I made a list of channels and what shows and days and times they were on. She reviewed that daily so she wouldn't miss any of them, another way of trying desperately to keep her in her routine so things were somewhat normal for her as other things around her were slipping away.

6. Patience

Patience would run thin when Mom would tell me something making perfect sense to her but not making any sense to me. We had a couple of times where she would get completely angry with me and if I said I didn't understand she would get angrier, then I would get impatient as well. It's those moments you need to step back, take yourself completely away from the situation, clear your head and revisit that topic later.

I had one night that I'm not proud of, but my patience was running so thin that I left. Got in my car and drove off and it was about half way home I called her to apologize and she said "its okay Bethie, I know I don't make sense sometimes, I'm just glad you called and I'm hoping you come back to see me again sometime." My heart sank, I felt awful and assured her I was never leaving her like that again and from that day forward I never physically left her when we both were confused on what she was saying or needing. We both decided when these things happen in the future we would both agree to say out loud what was confusing at that time and visit it later, together.

Final thoughts -

Its strange how the brain works when dementia is involved, some days are clear and others are so cloudy you don't know if you're coming or going when you are trying to have a conversation.

We had one day in particular that Mom was really cloudy, confused on most everything she was talking or asking about so we were having a quiet day trying not to make it worse when all the sudden Matt (my son who lives out of town) popped in for a visit. Matt and his "Gram" have always been extremely close so I knew it was tough for him to see her like that, but when he walked in the room it was like this switch clicked in her brain and she looked up at him, smiled like she always did when she saw "her Matthew" and the questions started flowing. "Matt, how are you? How's the new Job? How do you like Florida? How is your girlfriend?" They both giggled and talked for a good 15 minutes and she was back to "Gram" for him during his whole visit. It was in a sense like she was having that last "check in" with him before her departure to make sure everything was good with him. I've heard people do this at times when they know the end is near, guess we got our proof that day.

One of the biggest things I have realized is when I was dealing with Mom and she seemed scared or unsure, it was important that I remained calm and be sure to let her know that everything was fine and one way or another we would figure it out, even if on the inside I'm scared out of my wits and want to cry because the person in front of me wasn't truly my Mom anymore.

The most important thing? Keep that sense of humor. And listen, listen hard and if you need to take a step back for a minute because you don't understand what they are trying to tell you, it's ok. When Mom tells me something like, "I had a horrible time today getting the radio to work, every time I tried to talk I couldn't hear it and it just got louder every time I put it down" so I said hold on a minute I need to think on this" So, you couldn't get the volume on the phone to work in the earpiece, but the volume on the ringer is really loud now, right?" To which she replied, "Yeah, that's what I said" and yes, we had a good laugh on that one, I was starting to learn her "language."

And a heartfelt thank you to *you* Mom as I look back...

Now looking back on this a year after she has passed, what seemed like a horrible decision for me to make as her Medical Advocate and the trust she embedded in me with her final wishes, I feel I am totally blessed, grateful and amazed by her strength. I think her putting me in that position and as things really got scary was a gift because I know in my heart I did the best I could with what was put in front of me.

I made sure she got the best health care she could have, had her in the nicest facility I could find along with excellent care and love. What responsibility she granted me I wouldn't have wanted anyone else to have. Her remaining days as this "Monster" called dementia took control of her life, had her with the love of close family as well as the love from people she met only a few short months earlier.

Thank you Mom for trusting me with handling the things that came up for you during and at the very end of your journey. I truly understand now "why."

ABOUT THE AUTHOR

I am a daughter who had the opportunity to help her Mom through the toughest part of her journey in what we call life. For that, I am forever grateful for what I have learned and how I look at life today.

Made in the USA
San Bernardino, CA
31 March 2016